Your Local Area
TRANSPORT

Ruth Thomson

Photography by Neil Thomson

WAYLAND

First published in 2010 by Wayland

Copyright © Wayland 2010

Wayland
338 Euston Road
London NW1 3BH

Wayland Australia
Hachette Children's Books
Level 17/207 Kent Street
Sydney NSW 2000

Editor: Nicola Edwards
Designer: Edward Kinsey
Design Manager: Paul Cherrill

British Library Cataloguing in Publication Data

Thomson, Ruth, 1949-
 Your local area.
 Transport.
 1. Local transit--Juvenile literature.
 I. Title
 388.4-dc22

ISBN 978 0 7502 6084 8

Printed in China

Wayland is a division of Hachette Children's Books,
a Hachette UK Company.
www. hachette.co.uk

Free downloadable material is available to complement
the activities in the Your Local Area series, including
worksheets, templates for charts and photographic
identification charts. For more information go to:
www.waylandbooks.co.uk/yourlocalarea
<http://www.waylandbooks.co.uk/yourlocalarea>

Contents

What is transport?

Transport is any kind of vehicle that moves people or goods from place to place. Different vehicles can travel on roads, across water or fly through the air.

 What vehicles can you spot here?

Trains and trams run on metal rails.

 What powers a tram?

A local look

★ **Which of these vehicles can you see around your local area?**

★ **List any other vehicles you have seen.**

cars

narrow boat

bicycle

van

motorbike

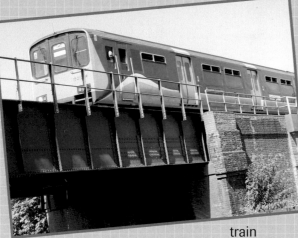
train

A vehicle chart

road	rails	water	air
cars			

★ **Make a chart listing all the vehicles you can think of that travel on roads, rails, water or up in the air.**

Travelling to school

Each day, thousands of children travel to school. Those who live furthest away come by car or catch a bus. Those who live closer to school can walk or go by bike.

 How do you travel to school? How long does your journey take?

school bus

walking bus

 What are the advantages of a school bus or a 'walking bus'?

A local look

★ **Describe your journey to school to someone. Say what you pass on the way.**

mosque

church

shops and cafés

petrol station

park

★ **Do a survey to find out how children in your class travel to school.**
★ **Display the results as a chart.**
★ **Ask children how they would prefer to come to school. Make another chart of the results.**
★ **What differences do you notice between the two charts?**

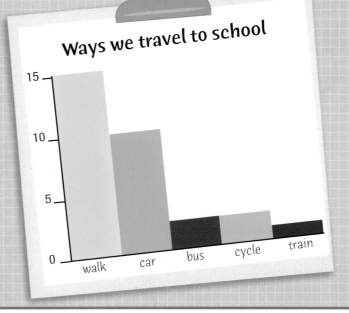

Ways we travel to school

15

10

5

0

walk   car   bus   cycle   train

Travel near and far

In the week, most people make regular short journeys to school, to work or to the shops. At weekends, they may travel further to shop in a city centre, to visit people or to play sport.

What journeys do you make daily, weekly and yearly? Does the distance affect how you travel?

A few times a year, people may travel a long way from home to visit distant family and friends or to go on holiday. They may get there by car, or perhaps by ferry, train or aeroplane.

A local look

★ Make your own diagram, like this one, to show where you go and how you get there from home.

★ Illustrate it with drawings or photographs.

My journeys

I go by car or bus to

clothes and shoe shops

the swimming pool

I walk to

the cinema

the park

the supermarket

a post box

my home

the local shop

the dentist

the takeaway

the library

the hairdresser

a football pitch

a railway station

Controlling traffic

The road signs and markings on most roads help control traffic flow and speed. There are also signs just for cyclists, buses and pedestrians. Traffic lights control traffic at crossroads and pedestrian crossings.

 What do red, amber and green traffic lights mean?

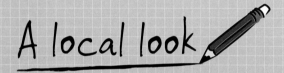

A local look

★ **Make a map of the roads around your school or home.**
★ **Take the map with you on a local walk. Mark on it any road signs, traffic lights, road markings and roundabouts.**

roundabout

Except buses and cycles
no right turn

30mph speed zone

Badgers
Watch out!
Badgers crossing

Road signs are different shapes and colours.
Signs inside circles give orders.

Signs inside blue circles tell drivers what they must do.

all vehicles must turn left

left bend ahead

Signs inside red triangles give warnings about the road ahead.

Signs inside red circles tell drivers what they must *not* do.

no entry for vehicles

end of cycle route

Signs inside blue rectangles give useful information.

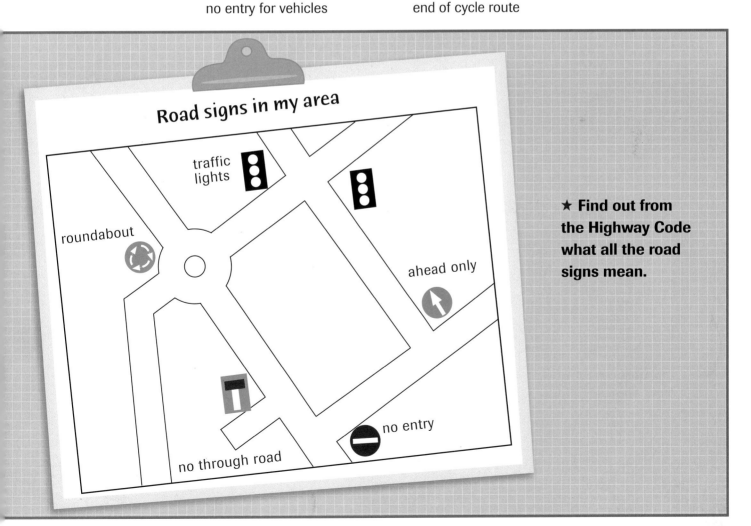

Road signs in my area

traffic lights

roundabout

ahead only

no through road

no entry

★ **Find out from the Highway Code what all the road signs mean.**

Finding the way

Drivers use sat-navs or road atlases to plot their route from one place to another. Road signs also help them find their way. Some direct drivers to a motorway, to towns and cities or to a car park. Others show distances to nearby towns or villages. Some signs show routes that only cyclists or pedestrians can use.

? Which of these signs are for drivers, and which are for cyclists, pedestrians or wheelchair users?

SIGN OF THE PAST

Milestones and mileposts at intervals along the roadside have distances marked on both sides.

In the past, travellers could discover how far they had already come on their journeys and how much further they still had to go.

In city centres, maps or signposts direct pedestrians to places of interest.

Some cities have roadside computers. People can use these to find out about local transport and plan journeys.

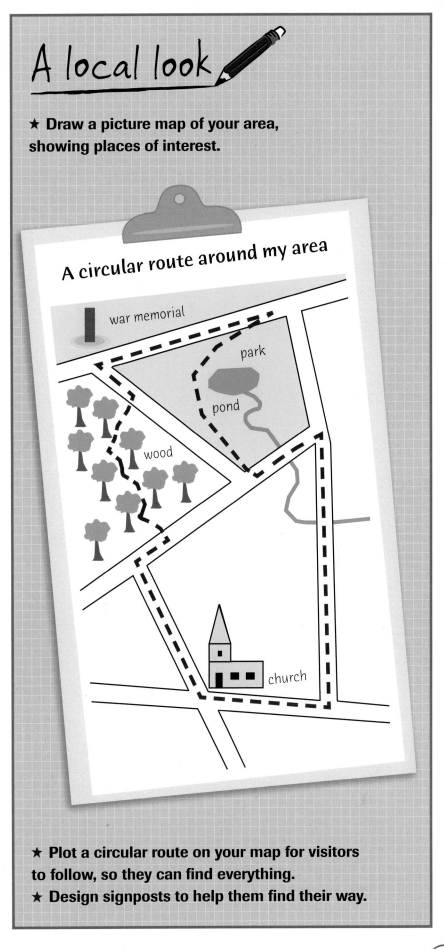

A local look

★ Draw a picture map of your area, showing places of interest.

A circular route around my area

war memorial

park

pond

wood

church

★ Plot a circular route on your map for visitors to follow, so they can find everything.
★ Design signposts to help them find their way.

How busy are roads?

Some roads are busy with traffic all day long. Others are busy only at rush hour, when people travel to and from work or school.

Traffic planners try to make sure that traffic on busy roads keeps moving. Vehicles are never allowed to stop on main roads called red routes and clearways.

CLEARWAY
NO STOPPING

Where can you see these signs and road markings in your local area?

red route road markings

A local look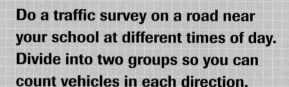

Do a traffic survey on a road near your school at different times of day. Divide into two groups so you can count vehicles in each direction.

A traffic survey

cars	lorries	bikes	buses	motor bikes
‖‖‖ ‖‖‖ ‖‖‖ ‖‖‖	‖‖‖ ‖‖‖	‖‖‖‖	‖	‖

★ **Make a chart like the one above.**
★ **Note each vehicle that passes in an agreed time, say 10 minutes.**

Compare your charts.
★ **Were there more vehicles going in one direction than another? Why?**
★ **Does the vehicle count change at different times of day?**
★ **When is traffic the busiest?**

Planners try to slow down traffic in residential roads to make them as quiet and as safe as possible.

road narrowing to stop lorries from entering

crossing island with two lit bollards

bollards mark the crossing point

green cycle lane with its edge marked with dotted lines

hump to slow down traffic

SIGN OF THE PAST

Before cars, trucks and the railways, roads were busy with horses, carts and animals.

When people went on long journeys by horse and coach, they stayed at inns along the way. Many of these still exist as places to eat or to stay.

Drovers walked cattle and sheep long distances along roads to market.

You can still find animal drinking troughs beside some roads. Now they are often used as flowerbeds.

Safe roads near schools

Fast traffic in streets near schools could be dangerous. Road signs warn drivers that they are nearing a school or tell them to slow down.

SCHOOL ZONE road markings remind drivers to watch out for children crossing the road.

? Which of these features are on the road near your school? Sketch the ones you find.

The school crossing patrol holds out his STOP sign to traffic at a zebra crossing near a school.

 Why is he wearing a bright yellow coat?

A local look

★Design some safety signs to put up outside your school to remind drivers and pedestrians about road safety.

Stay safe with Holy Trinity C.E. Primary School

ROAD SAFETY

LOOK CHILDREN

WATCH OUT KIDS ABOUT!

20's ENOUGH

Attention!

Learn LOOK Listen

Stop!

Tameside Metropolitan Borough

SureStart

Parking

People do not use their cars all the time, so they have to find somewhere to park them. Drivers cannot park wherever they like. Coloured lines on the roadside show if cars can park there.

What do these double yellow lines mean?

Resident permit holders only
Mon - Fri
11 am - 12 noon

How does this parking notice help residents find a parking place near their home?

Parking space is limited in streets of old houses built before cars were invented. Residents have parking permits, so they can park their cars in their street. Cars from elsewhere are not allowed to park there very often.

More modern houses often have driveways or garages where people can keep their cars.

When people go shopping, they often have pay for parking. Traffic wardens check that drivers who have paid at parking meters do not overstay their parking time.

Supermarkets, shopping centres, retail parks and DIY stores offer free parking for customers to encourage them to visit.

A local look

★ Find out what parking controls there are on the roads around your school.

No stopping
Mon – Fri
8.15 am – 9.15 am
11.30 am – 1.30 pm
2.45 pm – 4 pm
on school entrance markings

★ Look for both road markings and road signs.

★ Is there anywhere locally where people have to pay for parking? Why do you think this might be?

212

Closing the high street?

Town high streets can be very busy. There are often traffic jams. If town planners want to pedestrianise a high street, they have to find another route for the traffic. They also have to make sure shops still have access for delivery vehicles.

? What are the benefits and drawbacks of a pedestrianised high street for shoppers and shopkeepers?

A local look

Look at this map of a high street which has been closed to traffic.

★ What route does traffic take instead of going along the high street?

★ Where do workers park their cars?
★ Where do shoppers park?
★ Why is there extra parking on Saturdays?
★ How else can people travel to the high street?

★ How many bike rack spots are there?

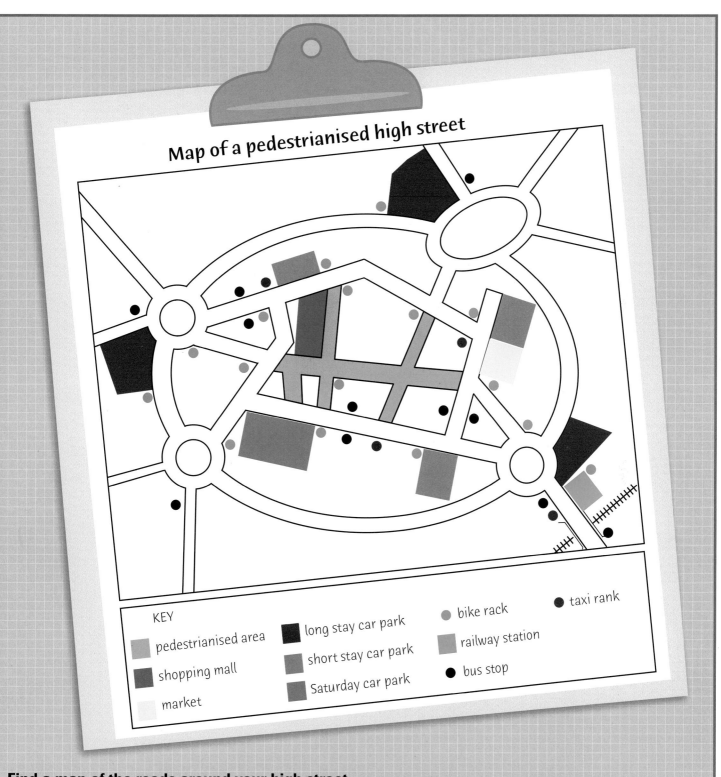

Map of a pedestrianised high street

KEY

- pedestrianised area
- shopping mall
- market
- long stay car park
- short stay car park
- Saturday car park
- bike rack
- railway station
- bus stop
- taxi rank

Find a map of the roads around your high street.

★ **Imagine you were going to close the high street to traffic.**
What route would the traffic have to take instead?

On the bus

Buses are always on the move, carrying passengers around town or from place to place.

 Why might it be better to travel around a town by bus than by car?

Signs on the front of a bus say where it is going. Most buses travel on a fixed route. Each route has a different number. The bus travels along the same streets and calls at the same bus stops on every journey.

sing

In big towns, there are separate road lanes for buses. Cars are not allowed to use these.

 Why are bus lanes a good idea?

In some places, buses will stop wherever passengers want to get on or off. These are called 'hail and ride' buses.

People who find it hard to walk can use dial-a-ride buses. These pick up people from home and take them where they want to go.

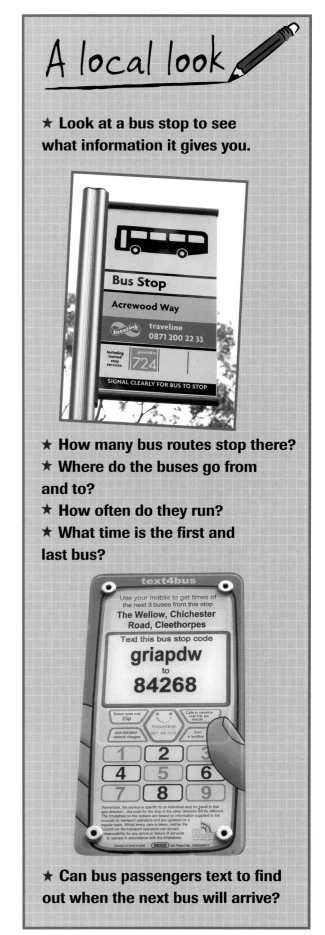

A local look

★ **Look at a bus stop to see what information it gives you.**

★ **How many bus routes stop there?**
★ **Where do the buses go from and to?**
★ **How often do they run?**
★ **What time is the first and last bus?**

★ **Can bus passengers text to find out when the next bus will arrive?**

Carrying loads

Trucks, lorries and vans transport heavy loads along main roads and motorways. They carry goods to and from ports, warehouses, factories, shops, building sites and homes.

Railways carry goods as well. Cranes lower containers of goods on to flat railtrucks. A locomotive pulls the railtrucks along the tracks.

? Do you think it is better to carry goods by road or by rail? Why?

A local look

★ Make a list of goods that these lorries, trucks and vans might transport.
★ Then list the places where you think the goods might be going.

Goods transport

vehicle	goods	place
tanker	petrol	petrol station

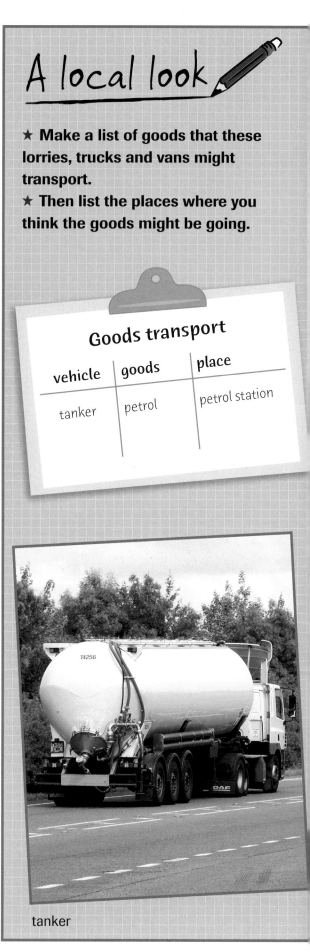

tanker

van

refrigerated truck

articulated lorry

skip truck

refuse truck

removals van

car transporter

Trains

There is a railway network all over the country. Trains run to a timetable, stopping at stations along the track.

Fast trains travel long distances between big cities. They have lots of carriages and make very few stops along the way.

Slower, suburban trains stop at every small station. People use them to travel short distances, for example, to work or school, or to go shopping.

A local look

Station

Visit your nearest railway station.
★ Find out where trains go to.
★ How many are fast trains and how many are slower stopping trains? What does this tell you about how the station is used?
★ How often do trains run to the city centre?
★ If your station has a car park, count the number of cars in it to see how many car journeys been saved.

The railway system developed in Victorian times. Many Victorian stations, bridges, tunnels and viaducts are still in use today.

a cast-iron railway bridge over a road

a brick road bridge over a railway line

Victorian stations had large clocks. Before the railways, time differed from place to place. Once the railways arrived, time was made the same all over the country.

More things to do

Look for these aids in your local area that help blind people or those in wheelchairs to cross roads safely.

Find road signs and markings near your home for one sort of vehicle, such as bicycles or lorries. Think why these signs have been put where they are. Take photographs of them.

Signs for bicycles

cycle lane

The pavement at many crossings is sloped for wheelchairs and prams. It has coloured, raised bobbles that blind people can feel underfoot.

Pelican crossings have a button at wheelchair height. Pedestrians press the button to stop the traffic.

A continuous beep tells everyone, including the blind, when it is safe to cross the road.

Push button
Wait for signal

Signs for lorries

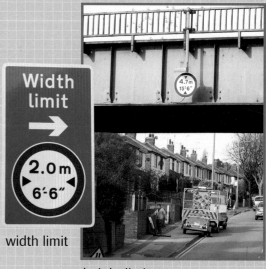

Width limit →

2.0 m
6'6"

width limit

4.7m
15'6"

height limit

28

footbridge

underpass

zebra crossing

traffic lights

traffic island with bollard

LOOK LEFT
LOOK RIGHT →

★ Which of these road crossings do you have locally? Do you have any others? What are they?

★ On what sort of road might you find footbridges or underpasses?

★ Is there anywhere in your area that needs a new safe crossing?

★ Write a letter to your local council explaining why this crossing is needed.

Glossary

access a way of getting into a place

articulated lorry a lorry with two separate parts – a cab and a trailer

bollard a low post on a pavement or road that stops vehicles from driving into or on to an area

bus lane a marked part of a road that only buses are allowed to use

drover a person who walked a herd of cattle or sheep from farm to market

inn a place to stay in the country

locomotive a railway engine that pulls railway carriages or wagons

motorway a road with two or three lanes for traffic going in both directions

narrow boat a boat used on canals, built to fit into the narrow locks

parking permit an official sticker that allows a vehicle to park in a place

pedestrian someone who walks on pavements or roads

refrigerated truck a truck that transports food and drink at a low temperature, so that they do not go off

resident someone who live in a place

road atlas a book of road maps

sat-nav (short for satellite navigation) a piece of electronic equipment in a car. It tells drivers which way to go, using information received from a satellite

school crossing patrol someone who helps children cross the road outside a school

skip truck a truck that lifts, carries and empties a rubbish skip

traffic warden someone whose job is to check that people have parked their cars in the right place and for the right amount of time

tram an electric bus that runs on rails on a road

vehicle a machine for transporting people or goods, such as a car, train, boat or aeroplane

viaduct a long, high railway or road bridge, often with arches, over a valley

Victorian the time when Queen Victoria ruled Britain – from 1837 to 1901

? Talking points

The questions in the book encourage close observation of the pictures and provide talking points for discussion.

Pages 4-5
• The picture shows cars, a single-decker bus, a coach, light goods van, crane truck and heavy goods lorries. Discuss what other vehicles children might see, including emergency vehicles, such as an ambulance, fire engine or police car. Children could collect pictures of vehicles or draw their own and divide them into those that carry people and those that carry goods.
• A tram uses electricity picked up by a pole on the top of the tram that touches overhead power wires. The electricity flows to controls, operated by a driver. The faster the tram needs to move, the more electricity needs to flow. Point out the pole and the wires in the picture.

Pages 6-7
• Discuss the benefits and drawbacks of different ways of coming to school. Cars can travel door to door and keep children warm and dry. A school bus can carry a lot of children at once - one bus uses less fuel than if the same children all came in separate cars. A walking bus gives children exercise, as well as reducing the number of car journeys to school, but may not be so popular in bad weather.

Pages 8-9
• Ask children to record the journeys they make in a week. Distinguish between the short, regular journeys they make to school, to the supermarket or to see friends and relatives from longer, more infrequent journeys for holidays and outings and discuss whether they use different methods of transport and the reasons for this.

Pages 10-11
• Encourage children to take a closer look at road signs, traffic lights and road markings, particularly those that control speed or keep pedestrians and bikes safe from traffic. All the signs are illustrated in the Highway Code http://www.direct.gov.uk/en/TravelAndTransport/Highwaycode/Signsandmarkings/index.htm

Pages 12-13
• The green road sign, crossroads sign and station/seafront sign are for mainly for drivers, but could also be for cyclists as well. The crossroads sign might also be useful for ramblers. The blue sign shows a special route for cyclists. The bus stop/station sign is only for pedestrians.
• Children could photograph or draw the different types of signs they see on a street and divide them into groups for drivers, cyclists and pedestrians.
• They could discover what different symbols on signs mean – such as those for an historic monument, a tourist office or camping and caravan site.

Pages 14-15
• Ask children whether they think where the school is situated is busy or quiet and to consider how traffic could be reduced.
• Take photographs of road calming measures and give each one an explanatory caption.

Pages 16-17
• Looking at school road signs and markings could lead to a wider discussion about how and where to cross roads safely, including how to use crossings, such as a zebra or pelican crossing. See: http://talesoftheroad.direct.gov.uk/stop-look-listen.php

Pages 18-19
• Carry out a parking survey of vehicles in a selected street at two different times of day and display the results on a chart.
• Discover whether parking is controlled and if so, how. Point out single yellow and double yellow lines and explain the difference between them. Discuss why a road might have double lines.
• Confining parking to residents between 11am and 12 noon prevents commuters, who might want to leave their cars for the whole day, from parking in this road.

Pages 20-21
• Children could take the role of different shoppers (for example a mother with young children and a pushchair, someone in a wheelchair, an elderly or blind person, a group of friends) or a shopkeeper and explain why a pedestrianised high street would be a good or bad idea for them.

Pages 22-23
• Discuss the advantages of bus travel in town. Anyone can take a bus so long as they have a ticket. Bus users do not have find somewhere to park. Buses are useful for short journeys if you have heavy bags. If more people travelled by bus than car, there would be less traffic, fewer road accidents and less pollution.
• Bus lanes speed up bus journeys, because the buses are not held up by other traffic.

Pages 24-25
• Freight trains can carry more goods in one journey than a lorry, but use the same lines as passenger trains and have to fit into a timetable. Lorries can carry goods door to door at any time of day or night. However, they increase road congestion and wear out road surfaces more quickly than cars.
• Children could each research a different type of truck and lorry, such as a breakdown truck, tipper, concrete mixer, brick lorry, flat-bed lorry, tanker, crane truck and rubbish truck, etc. and explain what they carry and what makes them distinctive and useful.

Pages 26-27
• Look on a map to discover where the nearest railway line is to the school. Follow the line to see what towns and cities it runs from and to.

Index